Rich Mum
Unknown Dad

Giuseppe Saturno

All rights reserved
Copyright 2024 Giuseppe Saturno
ISBN 9798303420236

This book is a work of satire.

Nevertheless, behind this unprofessional cover are things that are even too serious.

Any reference to real people or situations is NOT purely casual.

The author does NOT intend to offend anyone and disassociates himself from any form of discrimination, sexism or gender stereotyping.

The goal of this book is to make people think with a smile about important issues such as true wealth, and values in our society.

Translated form Italian!

Index

Introduction..5
Who is Robert T. Kiyosaki.................................7
   Here are the major criticisms......................8
Robert's key concepts..11
   Rich don't work for money...........................11
   Why teach financial literacy.........................18
   Mind your own Business................................24
   The history of taxes and the power of corporations..29
   The rich invent the money.............................44
   Work to learn-don't work for money...............58
During wartime, those who owned a pig were considered wealthy..64
The (real) way banks work....................................66
Let's go terraforming Mars!..................................71
Uncle Bill's Gardens...77
Insults and outrage..79
Seeds or ammo?..81

Introduction

Most people are born with a handicap that they will carry forever. This curse, in elegant words, concerns the lack of any "financial education," in other, less elegant words, they are born poor. And without any fault of their own.
Indeed, neither our parents, nor our school, nor our friends and acquaintances explain to us how money works and how to manage it. Imagine if banking institutions, those semi-legal entities that manage and create money out of nothing, explain it to us.
The result is that we carry this serious "gap" with us all our lives, making "mistakes" that will forever affect our existence.

This is more or less the meaning of what Mr. Robert, author of the best seller Rich Dad, Poor Dad, says.
And it certainly seemed to be the fate of Robert Kiyosaki, born into a family belonging to the American middle class in which the subject of money was even taboo. At the age of 9, however, little Robert has the "good fortune" to meet a kind of second father who will explain to him everything he needs to know to become a "real rich" person.
In addition to his real father (the poor father of the title), Robert will then also have a rich father from whom he will learn six essential lessons for achieving "success and wealth."

On the other hand, I had only one father, and besides being poor, he also had the handicap of being honest and educated.

In this book I would like to explain why I put so many quotes to these key terms, and summarize what I think we should tell our children before it is too late.

*I dedicate the book
to my grandfather
and my father.*

Who is Robert T. Kiyosaki

Robert Kiyosaki is an American entrepreneur, investor, financial educator and author, best known for his bestseller Rich Dad Poor Dad, published in 1997.
Born April 8, 1947, in Hilo, Hawaii, Kiyosaki is of Japanese descent and attended the U.S. Naval Academy, where he graduated and served as a helicopter pilot during the Vietnam War.

After leaving the military, he pursued a career in the corporate sector, working for Xerox before beginning several entrepreneurial projects. The turning point came precisely with the publication of Rich Dad Poor Dad, in which Kiyosaki recounts the influence of two father figures, "the rich father" and "the poor father," who represent the two opposing approaches to managing finances and investments. The book was an extraordinary success and marked the beginning of a series of publications on financial education.

Kiyosaki is also founder of Rich Dad Company, an organization that provides courses and content on personal finance, entrepreneurship and investing.
He has often promoted the importance of financial independence through buying assets and investments, such as real estate, stocks and cryptocurrencies.
However, his financial theories have also attracted much criticism, with some experts considering them risky for beginners.

These criticisms of Robert Kiyosaki mainly concern his investment strategies, statements, and his approach to financial education, which are considered controversial or dangerous.

Here are the major criticisms

Before we continue and delve into each aspect of Robert's best seller, let's see what experts believe are the main critical points.

Simplicism and riskiness of the advice
Experts point out that Kiyosaki's financial advice, such as betting heavily on real estate investment or "good" debt (i.e., using debt to buy profitable assets), can often be very risky for the inexperienced.
His insistence on using debt for investment is criticized because, if not managed properly, it can lead to significant financial losses, especially in times of economic crisis.

Unorthodox financial education
Kiyosaki promotes an unconventional approach to financial education, arguing that the traditional education system does not prepare people to achieve financial freedom. Although this idea is shared by many, his solutions (such as investing in speculative activities or abandoning the savings approach) are considered questionable.
We will see later how in reality all speculative activities can come to lose their usefulness completely.
Some critics also believe that his directions create unrealistic expectations, especially for those who are financially vulnerable.

Lack of hard data and real cases
In his books and speeches, Kiyosaki often does not provide concrete data or detailed financial analysis to support his claims, and his "Rich Father" character seems to be a fictional figure, which some critics interpret as an attempt to make his concepts more appealing without real foundation.
This narrative style, while effective for storytelling, has been criticized for not providing concrete and replicable examples.

In this book, however, I use the figure of my grandfather, who is far from fictional, and that of my father, who, if he were not there, would have to be invented. My reflections, although also lacking in numbers and tables, are also far from intangible and unfounded.

Promotion of paid courses and aggressive marketing tactics
The Rich Dad Company offers paid training courses that promise in-depth investment knowledge, but the high prices (with courses that can exceed thousands of dollars) have been criticized as exploitation of people seeking to improve their financial situation.
Some former participants have reported that the content of the courses is limited and that the main goal is to induce clients to purchase subsequent courses or more advanced programs.
This technique leads me to think of today's influencers, no matter the content, the important thing is to sell....
It also reminds me of **Charles Ponzi**, a famous Italian-American con man, who back in the 1920s stated that **"it is easier to fool people than to work honestly."**

I don't want to accuse anyone of being a con man, least of all Robert, but you also have to see things as they really are and try to have a complete vision.

Critiques from financial experts
Many financial industry personalities and business journalists have expressed skepticism about his teachings. **Forbes** magazine, for example, has repeatedly criticized Kiyosaki's ideas, characterizing his approach as overly risk-focused and unsuitable for the average audience, which may not have the tolerance or knowledge to handle highly speculative investments.

Robert Kiyosaki has had a significant and often positive impact in getting his readers to think about their finances, but his investment strategies, teaching approach, and marketing techniques remain undoubtedly controversial, especially because of the risks they pose to the underprepared.

Robert's key concepts

The book contains several chapters but there are 6 most important ones, each about an important teaching. Below I will summarize them for you by adding the necessary considerations to be made today, in 2025.
At the time of the release of Robert's first book, the Internet as we know it now did not yet exist, nor did cryptocurrencies, another topic among those covered by his later written books. Some of his predictions came true in the early 2000s.
Others did not.

Rich don't work for money

A nice little story expressing this concept is about Robert and his friend Mike, son of his wealthy father.
Robert and Mike, came from modest surroundings and due to territorial disposition found themselves attending a school where other children from a more wealthy class were studying.
While their classmates sported designer clothes and talked about exotic travel, the two friends felt increasingly excluded. Thus was born in them a curiosity to understand why some are rich and others are not.
Their fathers offered very different answers. Robert's father, a college professor, invited them to study hard to get a good job. Mike's father, on the other hand, an astute entrepreneur who was gradually building a fortune, preferred to teach them in a practical way.
Mike's father then hired them in his store. At first, the boys were disappointed by the strenuous and low-paid

work. But they soon realized that there was much more behind that simple activity.

One day, while working in the store, they noticed something strange: unsold comics were being thrown away. They ask for explanations and eventually get permission to take the unsold comics as long as they do not resell them. The two friends have the bright idea of opening a small library in the basement of Mike's house. For the price of 10 cents, which is the price of one comic book, young readers in the neighborhood would be able to access the library and read more than just one comic book.

Making this idea even more efficient was the fact that they decided to hire Mike's sister to supervise the customers.

Things were going well and they thought of opening a branch office, from that moment they were then faced with the well-known problem of finding "reliable staff."

This experience turned them into small business owners in their own right, and by the time they were only 9 years old, they were already facing one of the most familiar problems to those who run a store.

They learn how to run a business, solve problems and work as a team. Most importantly, they understand that wealth is not just about money, but also about creativity, initiative and the ability to seize opportunities. Unfortunately, the business was later closed due to a scuffle...

This is a brief summary of this chapter, but let us see what elements are never covered when discussing this famous book and are often left out or ignored in summaries.

To convey what drives ordinary people to stay poor and not get out of the "rat race," Mike's father uses the concepts of fear and greed. He explains that most people are terrified of running out of money.
And he is right.
In our modern Western world if you happen to be left on the street and without money, I wish you luck, because there is a great risk that you will die quickly if you don't adapt to the worst.
In other countries that are more civilized than ours and have other values, such as in the global south, or where poverty is greater, if you behave yourself you don't starve to death because there will always be someone with compassion who will help you with what little he or she has.
Not always, but in most cases.
Unfortunately, people without scruples hide everywhere.
Fear is that invisible force that drives us to do certain strange things, even very bad things.
And it is greed that makes us enter very dangerous territory for ourselves and our fellow human beings. Needless to say what we become capable of because of greed.

I agree with Robert in believing that these two feelings need to be understood and controlled, anyway.
If you're reading this book, you've most likely also already read the one by Robert, but I wonder if you've thought only about the chapter title or also about the concepts expressed later about education, work, the gold reserve, and... the carrot!

Let's go by order.

Once it was explained to the two children that they had to control these evil and harmful impulses, the rich father starts talking about education and its importance.
He refers to the fact that ordinary people, even if educated, do not have sufficient knowledge in economic and financial matters. That of financial intelligence will be the running theme throughout the book.

I would also add that education and knowledge are the best antidote against fear and greed.

Mike's father then adds that if they had not learned not to be afraid, they would have become slaves to money, like most people.
He also explains that they would be to blame, and not the state, the economy, or the rich.
This is actually where Mike's father begins to contradict himself.

After explaining a few concepts about taxes, and boasting that he definitely paid less than the poor father, little Robert asked why the citizens allowed the state to take first from the poor and then from the rich.
The rich father replied that it was really only the poor who allowed this, not the rich. He thus admits a certain cleverness in the way of the rich, who try at all costs to avoid paying taxes. The rich have learned how to do it; they have educated themselves.

They have learned how to take better advantage of a system. They have perfected the art of taking without giving.
This in my opinion is not education or useful

knowledge, it is something abominable.
First you talk about teamwork and then you take the side of those who sneakily profit more than others?
You talk about fighting greed and then try to cheat others?
I would be ashamed, just as my grandfather and father, who were both honest people, would have been ashamed.
I don't know if it will turn out to be a correct and sustainable teaching in the long run. But let's move on.

Again in order to explain to the two children that it would be better to be in full control of one's life, the rich father gives the example of the cart pulled by a donkey who sees only a carrot in front of him, and his goal is only to have a carrot every day.
He is obviously referring to the fact that from his point of view, the entrepreneur (or also exploiter of other people's time and labor) is in a position to go wherever he wants, while the donkey will only focus on the carrot.
Nice example, unfortunately we encounter, however, the first very very strong contradiction just a few lines later.

The indoctrination goes on to say that the rich create money and blah blah blah, but then states:

"[...] Rich dad went on to explain that the rich know that money is an illusion, truly like the carrot for the donkey. It's only out of fear and greed that the illusion of money is held together by billions of people who believe that money is real. It's not. Money is really made up. It is only because of the illusion of confidence

and the ignorance of the masses that this house of cards stands. In fact, in numerous ways the donkey's carrot is far more valuable than money."

And it is crystal clear that he is right, on this planet we live on water, food and clean air, not gold coins and diamonds. I wonder then if teaching the importance of money management is nowadays, in these current times, to be considered useless or even absurd.
I wonder if any parent who still teaches the absolute importance of money in today's social, environmental and economic context should be classified as a dangerous psychopath.

A few lines later Robert takes on an even more critical topic and begins to recount what his wealthy father explains to him about the gold reserve.
Many years ago, in fact, for every dollar created there was a corresponding one in gold or silver. Mike's father expresses in the story his concern about the fact that one day (which turned out to be August 15, 1971) this might no longer be certified and says:

"If that happens, boys, all hell will break loose. The poor, the middle class, and the ignorant will have their lives ruined simply because they will continue to believe that money is real and that the company they work for, or the government, will look after them."

I refer you to the chapter on how banks really work for more on the topic of money creation, in case you need to refresh your memory on the big idea of Nixon & Co.

Later in the text, and in the rest of the book, Robert also

gives us a very important lesson about instruction and education, which is also often overlooked and omitted by high-finance gurus and ignored by millionaire trainees.

Cito:
"History proves that great civilizations collapse when the gap between the haves and have-nots is too great. Sadly, America is on that same course because we haven't learned from history. We only memorize historical dates and names, not the lesson."

The two young boys then ask if prices should never go up, and the rich father's answer is this:

"In an educated society with a well-run government, prices should actually come down. Of course, that is often only true in theory. Prices go up because of greed and fear caused by ignorance. If schools taught people about money, there would be more money and lower prices."

If schools were teaching how to respect and cultivate the land, how to live a healthy life in harmony with others, how to consume fewer resources unnecessarily, how to understand history and how to appreciate the small joys of life, then yes, more vegetables would circulate and the rate of hatred, frustration and envy would drop.

But all this would then no longer appeal to the rich, wouldn't it Robert?

I refer you to the chapter "Uncle Bill's Gardens" to

learn more about carrots and whether there are any trees that produce edible money.

The chapter with the little story of the two children who work for 10 cents an hour concludes by explaining that we must try to see the things that others do not see, to know how to take the opportunities that pass us by our noses and that we constantly let slip away because of the obsessive pursuit of money.

Why teach financial literacy

In this chapter Robert focuses on the difference between assets and liabilities, and the importance of education (in his case, financial education, of course).
He wants us to understand which things really fall into one or the other category. As an example, he repeatedly insists that most people believe that the house is an asset.
In a sense he is right, and although everyone needs it, and in itself it creates neither money nor wealth, it is clear that in reality, owning a home also means spending money on maintenance, property taxes, and various bills.
A house or property really becomes an asset only if we are able to rent it out and make a steady income from it.
But the most curious thing about this chapter, in my opinion, is that to explain the difference between assets and liabilities, Robert gives the exact example of a tree. (And here my grandfather comes to mind again).
Robert gives several bucolic examples.
And I take this tree as my starting point to introduce what I think is a key theme when it comes to understanding the importance between assets,

liabilities, and the power of knowledge.

Have you ever heard of Permaculture?

If you have never heard of it, give me a few more pages and I will show you the parallels between what Robert's philosophy is and its equivalent in a truly sustainable world.

From this chapter on, Robert begins to use extremely simple sketches, so to make a good impression, I will do so as well.

So in the first sketch I will put the tree in the assets column, along with the sun, wind, water, and all the microorganisms that make life on this planet possible.

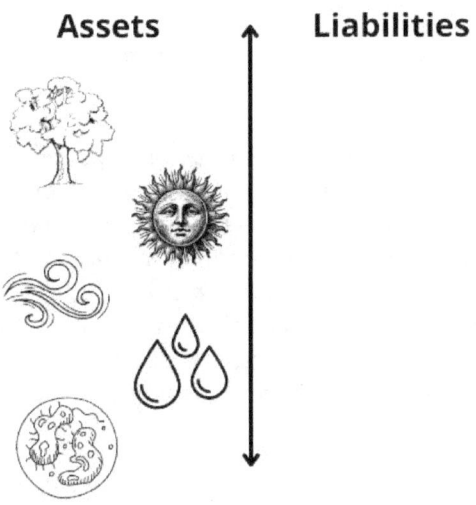

Robert uses the example of the tree to explain how certain things start to bear fruit constantly after putting time and work into them.

Exactly, in my opinion natural resources are the most important assets, they are already there for free.

After this example Robert introduces the next main theme of the chapter, which is education, stating that it is because of this that it is possible to maintain the wealth acquired. He always refers to financial education of course.
After giving the example of some very rich people who later died very poor, perhaps because of the famous crisis of '29, he also explains that today we are living in a time of much more drastic changes than those taking place in the 1920s and 1930s. (And imagine that he still did not know what would happen in the 2020s...)

I quote one of his contradictory passages that we will analyze in a moment:

"I suspect there will be many booms and busts in the coming years that will parallel the ups and downs these men faced. I am concerned that too many people are too focused on money and not on their greatest wealth, their education. If people are prepared to be flexible, keep an open mind and learn, they will grow richer and richer despite tough changes. If they think money will solve problems, they will have a rough ride".

And then again:

"Most people fail to realize that in life, it's not how much money you make. It's how much money you keep".

I swear to you that the first time I read these sentences,

I couldn't tell if Robert was making fun of us or if he didn't even know what he was talking about.
But didn't they say that with money you solve everything and get everything?
Listen, Robert, everyone who bought your book is looking forward to making the big bucks, and now you tell them that this will not solve their problems?
How should we read these statements?
Is there perhaps another key to reading them?
What is important, money or education?
Maybe both?

Okay, I'll try to give my interpretation of these at first glance rambling and conflicting sentences.

I start with the tree.
I planted the first tree in my life, together with my grandfather. I was very young and we were in one of his fields in Puglia.
He explained to me how to lightly compact the soil around the trunk, and he said we should water it frequently for the first two years.
I don't remember what kind of tree it was, and actually I don't even know where it is or if it still exists.
It was thanks to my father instead, that I lost contact with this tree. My dad, who is a bit like Robert's poor father to me (while my grandfather represents the figure of the rich father), needed liquidity and therefore sold grandpa's land.

I don't remember what exactly that money was used for. It was probably used to help us survive until today, certainly to give us an education, but of the tree I have no more news.

I can count myself a lucky person to have received an education and background that few can pride themselves on, and I have tried to this day to understand why my father had to sell that tree.

My grandfather was certainly the least educated of all, if we compare him to my father and me, but he knew how important that tree and his land were.

He was the least educated of all, but a few years later, from the countryside of southern Italy, he came to have a shoe store in downtown Milan.

This sign roamed through the house for several years but now I don't know where it ended up, since we didn't own a house, we had to dispose of several things, even family memories.

According to Robert, home is a liability, but in every way, it is that thing that allows you to live and thrive in peace, to store memories and bags of almonds, that thing that gives you comfort and protects you from the weather, that thing where a family, a group, a community grows and lives. We will also return to these concepts shortly.

And just going back to Permaculture, we see how both the **house** and the **tree** can instead be regarded as assets. We see how **knowledge** can be that thing that improves our system. We see how the group can be that thing that grows with and because of the system. We see how in a **well-designed and functioning system** there can be only assets and not even a liability.

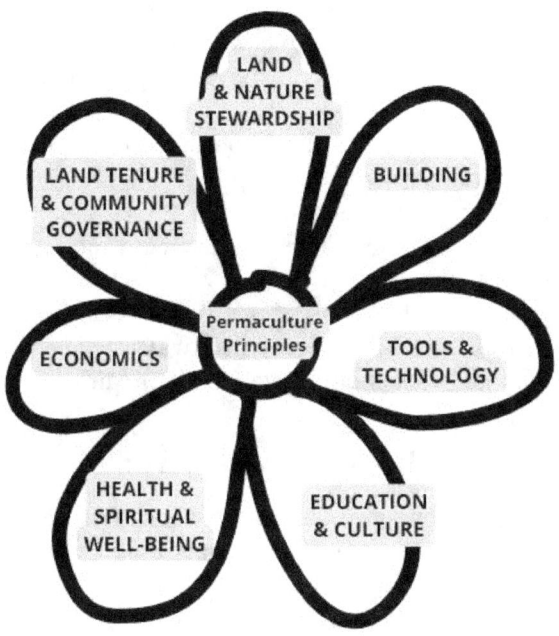

*The Permaculture Rose,
a very powerful financial tool!*

Speaking of groups, I quote a sentence toward the end of the chapter:

"An intelligent person hires people who are more intelligent than he is".

Here I am not thinking about intelligence or education, which we have already talked about, but how necessary people are. Having the right people around is really important, no matter if we have to pay them or if, better

yet, they are other members of our community.
The assets column of people who cannot afford to pay anyone includes good friends, preferably with useful and specific knowledge, helpful, selfless, able to relate socially, and aware of the importance of a group and their importance within a group.
The right people are assets.
A soloist, even one who is loaded with money, alone will go nowhere.
If you believe that you alone can buy and rule the world, remember that you will always need someone else who knows something you don't or can't do.

Mind your own Business

This chapter contains the sentence I hate the most in the whole book. And in this sentence is concentrated precisely the essence of one of the things I dislike most, selfishness.
I will quote it to you, then we will analyze it together:

"To become financially secure, a person needs to mind their own business."

That's horrifying.
First of all, I start by saying that these self-made people who have achieved success and are now bragging about their position only got there through scams, cheating and/or taking advantage of very poorly made laws. Those who try to work honestly, on the other hand, are no longer jerks. Those who pay taxes are no dumber than others. But taxes, or rather tax evasion, will be discussed in the next chapter.

These heroes of finance, these selfish, smiling tycoons, may not have realized that on their own, in a properly functioning society, they would not have it easy. In an evolved and fair society, they would be singled out as evildoers, as people to be kept away from because they take advantage of their fellow man.
I hope the meaning of the title of this book is now fully understood....

Taking care only of oneself and thinking only of oneself is not a good thing, it is not elegant, and it is also not a very smart move....
In the list of 8 things that Robert thinks the wannabe superman should occupy himself with, there are 7 that are nothing more than unreal, airy-fairy things that do not actually exist. Here they are all mentioned below:

1. *Businesses that do not require my presence I own them, but they are managed or run by other people.*
2. *Stocks.*
3. *Bonds.*
4. *Investment funds.*
5. *Income-generating real estate.*
6. *Notes (IOUs).*
7. *Royalties from intellectual property such as music, scripts, and patents.*
8. *Anything else that has value, produces income or appreciates, and has a ready market.*

Points 2, 3, 4, 6, and 7 are assets, standing only because of some very recent laws, and they are not part of the real world anyway. They also implicitly require someone else's work.

Point 5 makes sense only if we assume that there can be someone who owns more than one house, and also those who are forced to pay for a roof instead.

On point 1 I partially agree, and in point 8 we find precisely natural assets.

In fact, as I explained in the previous chapter, in my opinion the only real assets are the things that Nature provides us with. However, if even here, dear Robert, you tell me that you would rather play golf than tend your vegetable garden for a few minutes a day, you are not making a good impression. Is it possible that it sucks so much for you to make a living from your own strength?

I'm joking of course, Robert, I know you would never steal and you would never hurt anyone, but these brilliant ideas of living off your income, rest on some dubious laws that are part of a pretty rotten system.

You see Robert, taking care of oneself really should also mean taking care of others. If I try to be selfish myself for a moment, it occurs to me that if my neighbor smiles at me when he sees me, the quality of my life will also improve. If my neighbor is doing well, he will be happy and won't come to me to borrow anything.

And about point 5 I will give you an example: in the abandoned village in Spain where I live, all the houses were built with bare hands with the help of all the neighbors. Self-building is what was always done.

The idea was that everyone helped everyone to have a house. No one had to rent it because everyone had one. And every house was built with everyone's help.

Plain and simple, right?

By the way, for those who are interested and are able to cooperate and handle human relationships in a healthy way, there are still a few vacant houses in my village, for free.
Please refrain time wasters and would-be speculators.

Also about knowledge and education: it is better to spread it. It is counterproductive to do like those people who hid books or burned them.
Imagine if you were the only man in your country who knew how to fix the tiles on your roof: on the day you are in bed with a fever and no one is able to fix the ones on your roof, do you let the raindrops penetrate and fall on your forehead?
This is the reality, we will always need someone, we will always need knowledge that we don't have. Life is about interactions with the people around us.
A diagram?

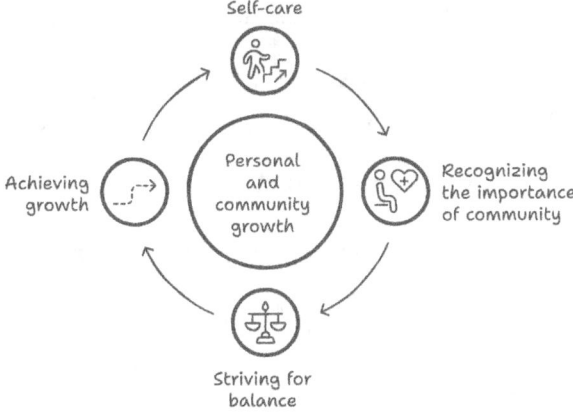

I personally like to help others and make my knowledge available. And if I had children I would teach them all the most useful and concrete things possible, not hiding behind clauses, contracts, unfair laws, and paperwork.

True prosperity is achieved by cooperating and seeking harmony with the environment and our neighbors, not by studying economics and finance.

I close this chapter with a small announcement: guess what, it's a house that takes care of your business! Amazing, isn't it?

Few people know it; it is called **Earthship**. If you want more information, Google it or go to New Mexico to visit them.

What I wanted to tell you is that architect Michael Reynolds, the inventor, when he realized that he had built a truly sustainable and self-sustaining house exclaimed, "**I am completely free!**" And he was right.

He was not free because he owned stocks or fixed incomes but because the house he designed and built was able to "monetize" natural assets by zeroing out the expenses of rent, light, heating, drinking water, sewage...

Take it from me, take a look at it.

There is also a movie about it: "**Garbage Warrior**".

Michael Reynolds, one of my heroes.

He knows how to capitalize on natural assets without destroying the planet or exploiting people.
He has created a community of happy, almost self-sufficient people. Almost like Robin Hood.
But we will talk abundantly about Robin Hood in the next chapter....

The history of taxes and the power of corporations

This is without a doubt the most repugnant chapter in the whole book. It is an insult to honest people.

I'm not mad at you Robert, but it's just that you are instigating people who behave well to commit barbarity!

Do you really think that everyone who has read your book has become rich?

I think you're just bragging about things you should be ashamed of, and you're instilling some very evil ideas into the heads of good people who, like Robin Hood, have much nobler ideals and values than you and everyone like you.

Excuse the somewhat sustained tone, but in reading this chapter I felt personally offended.

Anyway, don't worry, I'll calm down now and start by clarifying a couple of points that may not be clear to the potheads who have lost touch with reality:

- ! Taxes are essential to finance public services such as schools, hospitals, infrastructure and security. They are a **fundamental pillar of a civilized society**.
- ! Taxes enable the state to **provide collective goods and services** that an individual could not afford.
- ! Those who pay taxes with difficulty **deserve respect and support**. The tax system should be fair and progressive, ensuring that the load is distributed **fairly**.
- ! Those who evade taxes take resources away from the community and **harm the system**.
- ! Taxes are necessary for the common **welfare**. Those who pay them actively contribute to society. Those who evade taxes harm it.

So remember, dear Robert, that when you are riding down the road in your Porsche, you are using a road that was built with the work of many other people, long

before you had the Porsche.
I had a little diagram in mind but let's leave it at that, I think everyone understands and appreciates these basic points.

The basic idea that hovers in this chapter is that according to Robert, or according to his rich father, if taxes exist it is because of the poor and middle class. In fact, at the beginning of the chapter the history of taxes is told, from their introduction to the present day. It seems that at first they were introduced to "punish" the rich, and thanks to this slogan they were accepted by the masses who voted for their introduction.
So according to the rich father, it is because of the romantic ideal of Robin Hood that now the rich, unfortunate people are forced to circumvent taxes.
It's kind of like saying, "If you hadn't taken to the streets to demonstrate, you wouldn't have gotten a police truncheon and lost an eye because of a blank bullet."

Now, since I don't even know where to start, I'll just quote the offenses and barbarities one by one and comment on them properly.

"[...] the passage of taxes was only possible because the masses believed in the Robin Hood theory of economics: Take from the rich, and give to everyone else".

What do you mean with "believed"? Is it perhaps also dealing with manipulation? Even without social media?

Then it continues:

"The problem was that the government's appetite for money was so great that taxes soon needed to be levied on the middle class, and from there it kept trickling down."

All right that within government (among politicians) corruption has always been at home, but it seems to me that those with the greatest appetite have always been the rich, or am I wrong?
It is not clear since when exactly there has been a marriage of politics and corruption (or even mafia) but I am comforted to know that there are exceptions as well.

Look at this man for example:

His name is José Alberto "Pepe" Mujica Cordano, former Uruguayan president, former guerrillero and farmer.

Another one of my heroes.

He is famous (but not as famous as other politicians) for doing several positive things during his rule, but mostly because he was not only not corrupt, but also donated 90% of his salary to important causes.

Observe his smile and happy expression.

Look for some of his speeches.

Mujica is considered a noteworthy world leader, and was crowned "world's best president" by Monocle magazine in 2012.

His story was also documented in the biographical film "El Pepe. A Supreme Life" by Emir Kusturica, which was screened at the Venice International Film Festival in 2018.

Sorry if that's not enough.

But let's get back to the barbarities.

Still on the subject of the introduction of taxes, we read:

"However, the rich saw an opportunity because they don't play by the same set of rules".

It is precisely a sign of civility and respect to follow the rules we like best, clearly. Then the thugs are the ones like Robin Hood....

"The rich knew about corporations, which became popular in the days of sailing ships. The rich created the corporation as a vehicle to limit their risk to the assets of each voyage".

Ah, the days of sailing ships! What a nice neat way to call invasions and plunder!

"If the ship was lost, the crew lost their lives, but the loss to the rich would be limited only to the money they invested for that particular voyage".

This calls for applause. Truly, such cleverness and shrewdness I did not expect. What a brilliant idea to sacrifice poor people. How nice to gamble with other people's lives.
And then the crook is Robin Hood.

"It is the knowledge of the legal corporate structure that really gives the rich a vast advantage over the poor and the middle class".

Apart from the fact that you are admitting that you have a vast advantage over other people, which is unsporting, with this sentence you further demonstrate that your success is actually based on non-tangible things, on norms, rules and agreements. They are mental constructions; they have no physical existence. We will see later whether I would really recommend relying on these kinds of things.

Then Robert adds:

"It seemed to me that the socialists ultimately penalized themselves due to their lack of financial education. No matter what the "take-from-the-rich" crowd came up with, the rich always found a way to outsmart them".

Do they penalize themselves? I say instead that it is a lucky thing that not everyone has that kind of smarts and that they don't always just try to take advantage of others.

A really smart person should also think of others, not only of themselves. And it is fortunate that there are people who, instead of thinking about how to screw others and make them work for them, try to learn useful things, to engage in research, to use their genius to create useful and tangible things.

The rich father insists again and again that financial ABCs are not taught in school.

Fortunately! Imagine what would happen if everyone focused on finding legal loopholes to avoid contributing to society!!!

History, languages, geography, science and technology, music and even art should be learned in school. These are the things that are needed for a life worth living. These are the things that distinguish us from the animals.

(With all due respect to the animals).

...And so it was that by introducing taxes, the state became the great reservoir of money that it still is today, the great wagon on which many strive to ride, the comfortable cart drawn by donkeys.

In spite of corruption and other little problems related to the centrality of governments, it is not a bad thing that there is this entity that manages money. This makes it possible to pay pensions and salaries to those who work for the state and also, as mentioned at the beginning of the chapter, to pay for all the works needed by the community.

But there's a problem.

The rich with their factories also dip into these funds through government contracts.
And here we need to talk about the taxation system.
I'm not an expert, but summarizing it works like this: employees pay taxes when they receive their salaries, business owners pay them after reinvesting as much money as possible in the same company and paying for everything that actually serves their private lives (cars, lunches, phones, vacations disguised as meetings...).

"True capitalists used their financial knowledge to simply find an escape. They headed back to the protection of a corporation. [...] Using it, the wealth of the rich was once again protected ".

The financial knowledge.... ROFL....

Better to move on to the next barbarity: Plutocracy. A word that comes from the Greek, ploutos, meaning richness: the government of richness.
To me it seems crystal clear that those governing should be those individuals who have the gift of honesty and who know things. Those who have studied or know a certain subject should take care of it. Today, unfortunately, we see the most outlandish characters dealing with issues they know nothing about.
And still it must be said that the rich, who are mainly known to spend more time playing golf than in the library, take advice from people who have studied. They can buy the knowledge of those who have already acquired it. So they don't actually rule.
I give the example of foreign languages: a language is not something you can buy, you cannot acquire this kind of knowledge overnight.

You can pay an interpreter, that you can.
Knowledge of a language does not come with money, but with time and practice.
For example, to learn Spanish, it would be enough to spend a few weeks at Pepe Mujica's house.
There we would have a place to sleep and we could eat the delicacies grown in his garden, after helping him do all the necessary work, of course, it is not elegant to go to Mujica's house and mooch food.
And so, between a bucket of water and a basket of tomatoes, we could after a few weeks master the Spanish language. I imagine the scene, Pepe and I in his vegetable garden laughing and joking while at one point an industrialist with a briefcase shows up and offers us money to be his interpreter to talk about business with a neighbor of Pepe's.
And I imagine Pepe and I laughing at him at that point, "but excuse me, didn't you say you do everything with money? Why would you need us, use your financial sagacity!" And back down to laugh as we eat a nice corn and tomato salad and as the squire with the briefcase walks away offended.

Okay, let's stop dreaming, although it's nice and good for your health, and move on to the rich father's next insults against honest people.

"The problem is that the people who lose are the uninformed: the ones who get up every day and diligently go to work and pay taxes. If they only understood the way the rich play the game, they could play it too".

Except that loser there will be you.... And uninformed

too, since you have to come begging me and Pepe to be your interpreter!

Also, remember that those who get up every morning and go to work, maybe they have studied a lot (not finance) and are able to cure you of a serious illness! Oh, yeah, even Mr. Apple with all the trillions of dollars he had died young from pancreatic cancer, just like my father, who didn't have a dime, but at least enjoyed life longer...

And then tell me, you shrewd financial genius, do you think it is realistic to think that everyone can set out to do what you do? I think it is more real and feasible to think of a world where everyone works, learns, collaborates and supports each other.

A scenario where everyone wants to be "shrewd" reminds me more of the Wild West, it's a "every man for himself," a dangerous place where the one who shoots first survives.

On the other hand, I am not surprised that certain ideas come from the very people who live in the country where they erected a statue called Lady Liberty.

Liberty to buy firearms and to die in the streets without free medical care. Here in Europe at least you can't buy guns and basic medical care is (still) guaranteed to everyone.

"An employee with a safe, secure job, without financial aptitude, has no escape".

I guess instead the lost one is you, with your financial wisdom, but without any practical and useful knowledge.

In another silly book of mine, "Green Climate Future for you and for ME," where I talk about futile and abstract things, I proposed a fictional skit featuring Uncle Bill (I devoted a chapter to him later) and me, grappling with another gentleman with a briefcase...

I repropose it for you slightly readjusted:

Uncle Bill sits peacefully in his 20,000-square-foot vegetable garden, and he has the last remaining box of tomatoes on the planet that will allow him to live on salad greens for the rest of his days.

Then a well-dressed businessman arrives from outside, calls him over the intercom, and with a briefcase in his hand signals that it is full of bills and that he wants to buy half a crate of tomatoes.

Bill immediately makes a very rough estimate: considering that the briefcase has a length of 46 cm, a width of 33 cm, and a height of 10 cm, he uses these dimensions to calculate the available volume inside the briefcase, that is, 15.180 cm^3. Assuming that the bills are $100 bills that are about 0.11 mm thick and dividing the available volume in the briefcase by the thickness of the bills, you get the approximate number of layers of bills: 1,380,000. Then assuming that each layer contains 100 banknotes, then multiplying the number of layers by 100 gets the total: $138,000,000

A very impressive treasure! The scene ends that Bill, laughing, sends the shrewd entrepreneur packing.

Ultimately, in case it was not clear, the analogy highlights the dynamics of power, influence, and access to resources that can exist in the real world among people with different levels of wealth, knowledge, and financial power.

End of the little story. (Don't waste time redoing the calculation, it's made up).
Let us continue.

The next two quoted passages demonstrate very well the absurdity and incoherence of the message that Robert and his rich father try to convey:

"[...] That is why I believe that the idea of "take-from-the-rich" backfired on the very people who voted it in".

...And then:

"Every time people try to punish the rich, the rich don't simply comply. They react. [...] They hire smart attorneys and accountants, and persuade politicians to change laws or create legal loopholes.".

Do I dream or am I awake? Is it me who doesn't understand or have I missed some passages? Yet I seem to understand what I read, normally.
That is, according to him, even after admitting that the rich bribe those who should be doing the interests of all, he persists in saying that it is the poor's fault that they are poor?
He is openly confessing the crime of corruption, or am I wrong?
Would this be a lesson to pass on to your children?
Oh, Robert, did you proofread the book at least once before you published it?

And it doesn't end there, in the next few pages we reach the highest level of schizophrenia, check this out:

"During all the years I studied and learned from him, he always reminded me that knowledge is power", riferendosi al padre ricco.

"Without that knowledge, the world pushes you around".

He obviously refers to financial knowledge, the only knowledge that allows him to exploit the work of others. After that, he jumps to the victim's side:

"If you know you're right, you're not afraid of fighting back." Even if you are taking on Robin Hood and his band of Merry Men".

The mysteries of the human mind and its convoluted reasoning.
After saying that it is normal to bribe politicians, does he think he is on the side of reason?
Fortunately, I feel like laughing and not crying.
I am glad that we are not all the same and that there are consistent and down-to-earth people. I miss the peace and serenity of Pepe's vegetable garden.
My friend Pepe, now retired but still taking care of his chores himself without having anyone work for him.

"As a young boy, I did not understand what rich dad meant by owning my own corporation".

And I'm sorry that you grew up Robert.
I mean, I'm sorry that you grew up with certain examples before your eyes. Children should play and

develop their instincts, rejoice in the beautiful things that only childhood can offer, not be exploited and underpaid by an unscrupulous capitalist. They should not have to work without pay and then come to believe that it is okay to exploit people the way they have been exploited.

If you had grown up in Uruguay, or in another country where democracy came on a tank, you would not have written this book and you would not be bragging about having people working for you.

Let's close this tiring chapter by listing what Robert and his super father think are the things worth studying:

- **Accounting**
- **Investing**
- **Understanding markets**
- **The law**
  - Tax advantages
  - Protection from lawsuits

About this last point, judicial protection (which among other things works thanks to everyone's taxes):

"We live in a litigious society. Everybody wants a piece of your action. [...] They (the rich) *control everything, but own nothing".*

Let me guess, the ones who always go looking for litigation are the poor, right?
And anyway you're wrong, as already said there are also people like Mr. Mujica and me who wouldn't know

what to do with your money, who would never buy a Porsche to speed on pot-holed roads, and who fortunately for you are neither aggressive nor vindictive.

Those who hide are just cowards.

His children should spit in their faces. This is what those who control everything and own nothing deserve.

I close the chapter by updating a sketch, strictly in Robert's style:

The rich/ corporations	The people who work
• Earn	• Earn
• Spend	• Pay taxes
• Pay taxes	• Spend
• Corrupt	• Still believe in justice
• Exploit	• Tend to help each other
• Manipulate	• Typically show empathy
• Benefit from shared resources	
• Don't contribute to the community	

The rich invent the money

In this chapter Robert first talks about the problem of people's lack of confidence and indecision, then about the fact that we need to look for solutions.
Throughout the chapter he also exposes us to his teaching game, the Cash Flow game.

According to Robert, those who are "successful" and enriched in life do so because of a number of qualities that are not cultivated in school: audacity, nerve, balls, bluster, cunning, recklessness and others.
School, according to him, does not provide the knowledge necessary to enrich oneself.
You see Robert, you grew up in a very strange country.
The actual discovery of your country came about because of the desire for gold, that is, avarice and the desire to get rich. The people who had always lived there were fine as they were and certainly did not use gold for financial purposes, but rather for artistic, religious or aesthetic purposes.
Then the worst people around at the time came from Europe, and they didn't use good manners to settle there where you live.
They didn't try to integrate with the local people, everybody knows that. The massacres then continued for years to the West, everybody knows that too, and just the Old West is still synonymous with anarchy and bullying. Here in Europe we really use to say "it's like the Wild West" when we mean a situation where the law of the fittest, of who shoots first, applies.
And then the black slaves came along.
Another good story this one.

So Robert, what I want to say is that maybe you've been a little bit used to thinking that education is of little use and that instead you get ahead because of Cow Boy qualities.

You also have the gall in your country to make people think that you are going to go and import democracy into the rest of the world.

Don't misunderstand me now, I don't mean that in your country there are only unscrupulous people, on the contrary. Those who invented Jeans, popcorn and Chewing gum deserve the respect of the world population.

As for schooling and real education, I think that there are other things that other peoples understood long ago that are much more important.

I'll give you a few examples, then we'll see if the modern Cow Boys and their infallible method and courage have anything to do with at least one of these:

Agriculture and farming:
Mesopotamia: The cradle of civilization saw the emergence of early agricultural techniques such as irrigation and grain cultivation.
Andes: Pre-Columbian civilizations developed advanced agricultural systems, terracing and domesticated animals such as llamas and alpacas.

Medicine and health:
Ancient Egypt: The Egyptians possessed extensive knowledge of anatomy and practiced mummification and developed surgical techniques and herbal medicines.
India: Ayurvedic medicine, one of the oldest in the

world, is based on a holistic approach to health and uses a wide range of medicinal plants.

Mathematics and astronomy:
Mesopotamia: The Sumerians developed a number system and used mathematics to measure land and predict astronomical events.
Ancient Greece: The Greeks took mathematics and astronomy to new levels, with figures such as Pythagoras and Ptolemy.

Engineering and architecture:
Ancient Rome: The Romans were masters of hydraulic engineering, building aqueducts and sewer systems that are still admired today.
Maya Civilization: The Maya built pyramids and massive cities, demonstrating advanced knowledge of astronomy and engineering.

Philosophy and law:
Ancient Greece: Greek philosophy shaped the way we think and reason, while the first legal codes were drafted in Mesopotamia and Ancient Egypt.

Also:
Wheel: Also invented in Mesopotamia, it revolutionized transportation and trade.
Writing, developed in different civilizations, enabled the transmission of knowledge and the birth of history.
Metallurgy: Metalworking led to the creation of more efficient tools and weapons.

These are the foundations of knowledge and are learned in school, which should normally be free and guaranteed for all, or do you have objections?

This knowledge accumulated in the past is the basis for all modern technological innovations.
Only by studying ancient civilizations can we better understand our history, values and identity.
It is also most important to point out that many of these discoveries are not attributable to a single civilization, but are the result of a process of **cultural exchange** and dissemination that **spanned millennia**.
These civilizations thrived without your financial teachings; indeed, problems appeared precisely with the industrial revolution, and our friend **Karl** predicted this.

These civilizations did not necessarily have to invent money, because they invented far more important things!

I don't know if it has much to do with this talk, but one last thing occurred to me about courage and resolve: A short time ago I was fortunate enough to be in northern Morocco and I went to see the coasts from where hundreds of people are trying to leave to get to Europe.
From those shores you can see Spain, but it doesn't seem to be very close; it's a distance that is still awe-inspiring.
There are so many causes for people to leave their land and risk their lives.
But tell me, you who have been in Vietnam for a good year, would you swim it from Morocco to Spain?
Would you give those who manage not to drown and make it to Spain a medal for civilian valor?
What do you say Robert?

Isn't it better to arrive in a country by swimming and with the intention to adapt and work instead of arriving by shooting, raping or spraying napalm early in the morning before breakfast?
End of digression.

Let us move on by quoting the next interesting passage that allows us to connect to our friend Karl, mentioned a few paragraphs ago:

"Generations from now, people will look back at this period of time and remark at what an exciting era it must have been".

The first thing that comes to mind when reading this very apt prediction is the face Greta would make.
Her eyes would widen and she would have an asthma attack. I hope she doesn't read it.
So, speaking of capitalism and future generations, Karl said:

"Every advance in capitalist agriculture is an advance in the art not only of robbing the workers, but also of robbing the soil. Every progress in increasing the fertility of the soil for a given period of time is a progress toward the ruin of the most lasting sources of that fertility."
Karl Marx, The Capital, I, sec. 4, ch. 13, §10

Translated into very simple terms, it means that by dint of inventing money, we have destroyed the ecosystem. And this is also reiterated by Greta who is still a minor....

"The development of capitalist production makes it constantly necessary to increase the amount of capital invested. [...] It forces the capitalist to constantly extend his capital in order to conserve it."
Karl Marx, The Capital, I, sec. 7, ch. 22, §4

It would not be a bad thing at all to endlessly increase the production of basic necessities; imagine a world where everyone has food, edible plants grow everywhere and no one starves, that would be nice. The problem is that capitalists are increasing their capital through CO_2, deforestation and pollution.
I honestly couldn't tell if they don't realize this or don't give a fuck at all.
Probably the second option, in fact:

"In every stock scam everyone knows that sooner or later the crash must come, but everyone hopes that it may fall on the head of his neighbor. [...] "Après moi le déluge!" is the watchword of every capitalist."
Karl Marx, The Capital, I, sec. 3, ch.8, §5

And as we know, Greta has noticed for a while that this is all falling on her own head. That's what the younger generation thinks about the exciting time you had, Robert. So much more than going golfing.

To me, it seems more and more evident that those who preach these kinds of theories of development and growth should have nothing to do with raising children. I would even take away their child custody if it were up to me. Unless you want your children to learn to commit crimes against humanity.
And anyway I repeat, the younger generations know

very well that they are going to be faced with very different problems from having to or wanting to create money.

"TIt was full of turmoil, and it was exciting", Robert continues a few lines further on.

Bravo. At least you guys had fun, I'm glad.

Karl, on the other hand, found nothing exciting about it even then:

"The need for a constantly expanding market for its products drives the bourgeoisie all over the surface of the globe. It must nestle everywhere, settle everywhere, establish connections everywhere."
Karl Marx and Friedrich Engels (1848), The Manifesto of the Communist Party, Ch. I, §18

And that means only one thing: trains, planes, trucks, and poor people on bicycles expensively transporting shoddy goods around the world.
Needless to elaborate, you all know this is a very big problem. And in the meantime, Robert and his friends enjoy playing golf.
It is probably on a Green that they came up with the idea of inventing a game and then charging players to play it. Amazing how they manage to squeeze money out of people in any way.

The Cash Flow Game
In this chapter Robert, who has been traveling the world for years giving lectures on "how to get rich," describes a game of his own invention, the Cash Flow

game. Apparently it works, but we do not know how many people have actually become billionaires through this game.
In the book it is not clear exactly how it works, perhaps with cards being drawn.
In any case, I think the fact that really matters is that you pay to play.

Even I, in the lectures I give about self-sufficiency, bio-construction, Permaculture and other such crap, I always propose to play a game to explain that it is actually very easy to get out of the rat race in an elegant, sustainable and social way.
I call it the Life Flow game. It is free, since I am quite an idiot compared to Robert.

My game consists of having the participants place themselves in a circle and establish that each of them represents an essential aspect of life.
Now, since the main problem of the poor in getting out of the rat race is that they have to sweat every thing

they consume or need, the outer circle represents the chain of paid goods and services.

To simplify, I have put only 7 basic aspects in the following example: home, health, education, food, transportation, technology, and recreation. It can usually be adjusted depending on the number of participants.

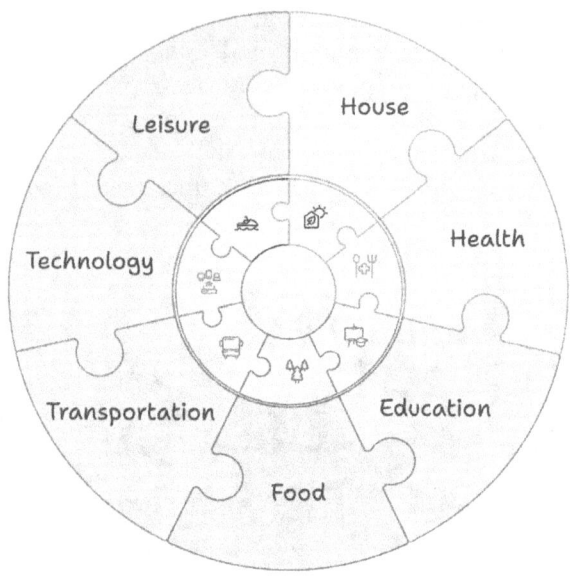

So consider that in the outer circle are goods and services that we are obliged to pay for: it's a vicious circle, and even though you get a free house, there are still the other things left to pay for.

So you still have to go to work.

So this does not allow you to leave the rat race and will force you to remain tied to that (capitalist) system so loved by those who take advantage of it, and so hated by those who are slaves to it.

Robert's version of the game involves him giving symbolic gifts, a boat for example, and seeing how the players react.

Now, continuing the game, the person representing the house moves to the center of the circle, and begins to make up the circle of guaranteed goods and services at no monthly cost.
At first he will be lonely, it is clear, although he lives in his own house, has no food, cannot move, and has no one to rely on.

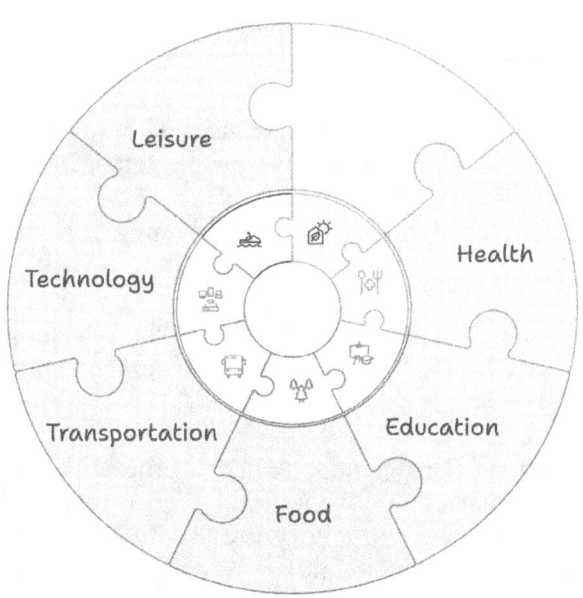

To make a long story short, in turn, each person thinks about how he or she could procure each of the needed goods and services and tries to move to the inner circle.
The person representing technology, for example, might say, "I can provide free house maintenance in exchange for a room."
And again, "I can take care of the vegetable garden and greenhouses."
"And I provide my car."
Thus self-sufficient communities are born.
Or at least, clusters of people are born who will emerge from the tunnel of exploitation and the mathematical impossibility of thriving.
Indeed, when all aspects of life have shifted to the inner circle, little will be left to achieve independence and happiness. Remember what Michael said about Earthship?

And it is also nice to observe that as the inner circle becomes more populated, the people left in the outer circle will look forward to being part of the one where things are good, too, and will do anything to be part of it.

This game is an example to show that one does not actually have to invent money, but to get the things one buys with it.

WARNING. This game is very dangerous and the rich and politicians don't like it at all! Who would work in their factories if everyone lived happily in interconnected communities? Who would consume their useless products? Who would rent their houses bought at auction?

So in case you decide to join other brave people with tangible knowledge, you have to expect repercussions of various kinds.
There are already several networks to get in touch with the inner circle, just look for them. Avoid social media though, those are full of informants, trolls and people who will waste your time.
As already mentioned, there is still room in the village where I live, applications are being accepted.

Well, games aside, let's go back to reading the next few pages and see what else Robert tells us.

"Land was wealth 300 years ago. So the person who owned the land owned the wealth. Later, wealth was in factories and production, and America rose to dominance. The industrialist owned the wealth. Today, wealth is in information. And the person who has the most timely information owns the wealth. [...] There will be a dramatic increase in the number of new multimillionaires. There also will be those who are left behind".

Exactly! Great Robert, you really predicted it very well! Long live equality, long live the Wild West!
You see, actually even today those who own land are rich.
In fact, he who owns land is richer than those who own stocks.
You later in your book cite Bill Gates as an example of an innovative entrepreneur; I spent a whole chapter on him.
You couldn't know it, but now Bill owns so much land, so much. And also about real wealth I wrote a chapter.

But before I go on let me comment on this sentence, which is also fascinating:

"I know people who are losing their jobs or their houses, and they blame technology or the economy or their boss. Sadly, they fail to realize that they might be the problem".

Again with the story that the poor are to blame?
In the previous chapter you already said such a barbarity, now listen to what Karl said:

"The improvement of machines not only demands a decrease in the number of adult workers employed to achieve a given result, but substitutes for one class of individuals another class, a less skilled class for a more skilled one, children for adults, women for men."
Karl Marx, The Capital, I, sec. 4, ch.13, §205

Why do you think the poor are the problem? Do you think it's because they don't work better than machines? You obviously couldn't have known that when you wrote "rich dad, poor dad," maybe because you have never read Marx. I know that in your country certain philosophers do not come across as very pleasant, but you said it yourself that information is important, maybe if they had let you free to read certain books like The Capital instead of censoring them, which is typical of a free country, you would have thought twice before writing such things and offending honest people.

In any case, reality has exceeded even Karl's predictions; today there are Robots that do almost everything, you just have to teach them. And not only that. They don't complain, they work even at night, they don't go on strikes, they don't smell, they don't get sick, and they don't even know what workers' rights are. The perfect workers!

That is why, especially in America, a country where workers' rights, social protection, health care, pensions and unemployment compensation seem to be science fiction, many people sleep on the streets or in tent cities.

Not because they are stupid.

Maybe they are just more honest.

I don't know where this will lead. We don't know, but we sense, that this mad rush for endless growth will bring no good. It has already happened to many civilizations to collapse because of too high divergences between classes.

And the most ridiculous thing is that even the rich dad has already said so! On page 17, to be exact, I even quoted it, but probably Robert, writing the last chapter, had forgotten it.

And anyway, these are things you learn in school, so who cares.

"The bourgeois relations of production and exchange, the bourgeois relations of property, in short, modern bourgeois society, which has as if by a spell produced such powerful means of production and exchange, is like the sorcerer's apprentice incapable of controlling the subterranean powers he himself has conjured up."
Karl Marx and Friedrich Engels (1848), The Manifesto of the Communist Party, Ch. I, §29

The chapter goes on to give a couple of practical examples of how to speculate with real estate, so I, too, agree with Robert's advice: Guys, go jogging with $20,000 in your pocket, you never know, you might find a cottage to buy at a bargain price!

Work to learn-don't work for money

This chapter on the other hand is much more likeable to me, I like it already starting with the title. I like learning, and I think it is very important to keep learning useful things throughout life. By now, dear readers, you should have understood, I believe that knowledge is much more important than money.

Robert, on the other hand, while admitting that he has studied subjects other than finance, persists in saying that school and academic knowledge is of little use.

It seemed too good to agree with Robert on at least one point; in fact, reading the chapter, one realizes that the title should be interpreted in another way.

Everything is about marketing, about sales.
According to Robert and many other forward-looking businessmen, it is not the content or essence of things that is important, it is not their value or their usefulness that is important, according to a capitalist what matters is selling.

At the beginning of the chapter, Robert describes his encounter with a journalist who, despite being a professional in the field of writing, could not sell her novels.

Robert clearly advises her to take courses and learn the art of selling. The journalist takes offense, saying that she was a college graduate and had skills of a certain level, and that she would not stoop to having to learn the techniques of manipulation and creating needs (this is marketing).

And she was right to be angry and offended. Today we are at the mercy of very ignorant people who respond only to the call of money. Our society is drifting because of this mentality.

But let's carefully analyze the situation.

As mentioned above, we live off goods and services, and these are more or less common to everyone, regardless of race, age or gender.

They represent our survival and can even make our lives complete and satisfying, if we are satisfied with them.

Everything else is superfluous stuff, or luxury.

Thus, there is no real need to advertise these products because it is clear that there is demand, and there will also be supply as long as someone specializes in producing and providing such services and goods.

The need to convince someone to buy something is when what we want to sell is not really of primary necessity, which is why we talk about induced needs when we refer to the hammering supply of useless products.

It is also because of these useless products that the rich make money, and to get you to buy them they need marketing.

In an ideal society, not ours nowadays, everyone has a task and everyone integrates seamlessly into the social fabric by bringing his or her knowledge, intellectual or practical.

However, Robert insists that specialization prevents making money and that it is better to have notions of varied subjects. To explain this he gives the example of a pilot with 10,000 hours of flying time who suddenly gets fired. He will not find another equally paid job because his knowledge is too specialized.

On the one hand, I can agree with him. For instance, David Holmgren, a pioneer of Permaculture, shares that in his Tasmanian village, everyone had multiple skills and held various social roles. This aligns with one of the Permaculture principles, and in the aforementioned ideal society or small community, this is a significant advantage.

On the other hand, there are also areas where specialization is not only necessary but synonymous with reliability.

Robert, would you let someone who doubles as a mechanic and a weekend pizza chef at the pub operate on your liver?

In each of these cases, it seems to me that marketing serves little purpose: we know hospitals exist (as long as we continue to pay taxes and they don't privatize everything), and we know that mechanics and places to eat pizza (pizzerias) exist.

Depending on the level of expertise, I'll decide whether to visit a skilled mechanic or a less experienced yet more affordable one. The cost of their services will be determined by their availability and expertise.

Also, the "man in the middle" is no longer needed, and many are already working to remove him from every aspect of our lives.

If we shifted our focus from finance and marketing to learning useful skills, we wouldn't need to worry about selling them. These skills would provide immediate and tangible benefits, regardless of time or place. Do you recall the list of skills I compiled while discussing the previous chapter? Those are the things to focus on, not marketing...

...And now, it's time for advertising!

**Ever heard of Permaculture? Probably not, since the TV doesn't cover it.
Then don't hesitate to grab this book!**

Jokes aside, I'm suggesting this book not just to earn a few bucks from Amazon, but to offer you something that I believe can truly make a difference. And I swear, I'd much rather have the certainty of living in a world, or village, where people thrive and enjoy life in health and harmony, instead of writing motivational books to inspire others. This applies to both the Permaculture book and the one you're currently reading.

And that's the end of the advertisement.

Let's wrap up the chapter with one last sentence.
Robert claims to have found a middle ground between his rich and poor father, who was concerned about the growing gap between the wealthy and the underprivileged. He then reveals his socialist side, and states:

"I personally hold the archaic educational system primarily responsible for this growing gap".

It's likely a reference to the American school system, which makes me shudder just thinking about it.
But Robert, the problem is once again privatization.
If governments, under pressure from individuals like your wealthy father, continue to cut education funding, it's clear that these services will suffer in quality. Could it be that you haven't thought of it yet?
The school system deserves a separate book, but essentially, what happens in healthcare is mirrored in schools. Here in Europe, many public facilities have been sold off to vultures, leaving them inoperable.
We've blurred the line between the sacred and the profane.

And frankly, I believe it's a deliberate and intentional move to keep ordinary people in a state of ignorance and insecurity. This way, they'll accept any shitty job until they're eventually replaced by robots. I don't think any government is interested in enlightening the people on financial matters (and if you don't know what Mr. Ford said about it, do your research or read the chapter on how banks (really) works).

Some have even suggested, and Karl had also hinted at it, that soon there may be no one left who can afford the trinkets produced by robots, if no one has enough money.
However, this is part of the broader capitalist delirium.
Time will tell for those who remain.

During wartime, those who owned a pig were considered wealthy

This phrase is a popular saying that holds a profound meaning, tied to survival and the economy, not just in times of crisis. I first heard it from my paternal grandfather, who was too young to fight in the First World War and too old for the Second.
Thanks to the family's possession of a pig and other natural assets, they were able to share both the first and second wars with us grandchildren. I also recall that he preferred edible plants over flowers and ornamental plants on his land.

The idea of true wealth and well-being was quite different a few years ago. It was still associated with a job and a responsibility to be taken, something tangible and concrete. The rest was just trivialities, nonsense, as we would call it today.

The countryside has always been a source of security and genuine wealth for those who knew how to work it and reap its benefits. My friend Sitting Bull, in one of his most famous quotes, made this clear:

"When they've polluted the last river, cut down the last tree, caught the last bison, caught the last fish, only

then will they realize that they can't eat the money stored in their banks."

I'm curious to hear Robert's thoughts on this quote.
In reality, Toro's fundamental economic concept, which had almost nothing in common with Robert, was expressed. Perhaps the only commonality between them was their shared experience with a rifle, with Robert defending American 'rights' around the world, and Toro defending himself and his people from those who preached economic growth.
I understand that there are always more perspectives to consider.

What I don't understand is why we're so drawn to bullshit these days. Work is a pain, we can't stand up for ourselves, and we've lost sight of what's truly essential for survival.

The (real) way banks work

"It is well enough that people of the nation do not understand our banking and monetary system, for if they did, I believe there would be a revolution before tomorrow morning." - Henry Ford

And that's all I need to say.

The process of money creation by banks is a perverted and mysterious mechanism, at least for most ordinary people.
Initially, banks would issue banknotes after securing gold bullions in their vaults, granting them the right to print paper notes that held the same value as the gold they represented.
As mentioned in the first chapter, Nixon and his cronies decided it was best to grant banks the power to print as much as they desired.

In simple terms, banks have stopped printing banknotes for quite some time now, instead generating money by granting loans. This is made possible by the fractional reserve system, which allows banks to retain only a small portion of their customers' deposits and utilize the remaining amount to grant loans. Whenever a loan is granted, new money is injected into the system. This money can then be deposited in other banks, which will use it to grant more loans, and the cycle continues indefinitely.

This creates a chain effect, known as the money multiplier, which increases the amount of money in circulation.
However, these are well-known facts to Robert's readers, and I, being far from an expert on the subject, certainly cannot offer any new insights into the banking system. To provide a comprehensive overview, I wanted to explain this well-organized scam in my own words to readers who may not be aware of it.

Today, the banks' ability to create money out of thin air has also come under criticism, but in reality, no one would dare to take concrete action to stop this outrageous scam that has been going on for years. Some rightly argue that this is an excessive privilege, giving them an unfair advantage in the economy.
Banks have the power to determine who can access credit and under what conditions, thereby shaping investments, consumption, and ultimately, people's lives. This power only serves to deepen inequality, benefiting those who already have access to resources and leaving behind those who need them most.
Moreover, the excessive creation of money can lead to speculative bubbles and financial crises, causing negative consequences for society as a whole.

The tale of economic growth

As you know, I'm no expert on economics and banking, despite having read some enlightening books (I recommend *Sacred Economics* by **Charles Eisenstein**). However, when it comes to calling out the infamous and cowardly, I'm well-versed and confident.
Our economic and banking system is founded on the

absurd notion that growth should be perpetual and boundless.
To illustrate this concept, let's use a simple yet effective method: two images.

The first shows the planet brimming with resources...

...The second depicts the planet's economy at its peak of growth.

Fortunately, this absurd and harmful idea is being increasingly challenged, at least by a few thousand 'crazy rebels' like me.
On the one hand, infinite growth means an ever-increasing consumption of natural resources, which are limited and cannot be exploited indefinitely. On the other hand, economic growth doesn't necessarily translate into a general improvement in well-being. Instead, it tends to exacerbate inequalities, with wealth concentrated in the hands of the usual few artists of finance and individualism.
Ultimately, GDP, the renowned economic growth

indicator, completely disregards crucial factors such as quality of life, health, and the environment.
Chasing infinite growth is a perilous illusion, leading us to trade long-term well-being for fleeting progress.

A few years ago, the Austrian Chamber of Commerce coined a brilliant slogan: *"Geht's der Wirtschaft gut, geht's uns allen gut"* (When the economy thrives, we all thrive.)
However, the reality is quite the opposite.

The economy as we know it today, the one that generates money and depletes resources, will ultimately destroy us all.
Perhaps with the exception of a few wealthy bankers who, as the world fell apart, built an atomic bunker with greenhouses to grow potatoes, like on Mars.
Or like those filthy mafiosi who, despite all their money, live buried underground like worms.

Henry Ford

Let's go terraforming Mars!

As you're likely aware, for the past few years, the topic of colonizing Mars has been a hot topic everywhere. Some individuals are convinced of the necessity of colonizing Mars, and perhaps even other planets out there where breathing is impossible and not even a blade of grass grows.

The Mars Society, as it's known, is the most renowned fraternity of ambitious visionaries, united by a single goal: conquering the red planet.

And then there's the great Elon, who, of course, also has some brilliant ideas from time to time.

But why is this chapter about Mars and its future inhabitants so crucial?

When discussing wealth and resource management, it's crucial to start from the very beginning. And I'm reminded of the opening scenes of '2001: A Space Odyssey,' the iconic film by Stanley Kubrick.

I won't dwell on the meaning of this film, but rather on the fact that since the world began, living beings have always needed the same essentials to survive. For millennia.

Beyond wars and rivalries, every living creature on this planet requires resources.

Now, if you're reading this book, chances are your parents taught you that money is a necessity for life, otherwise you'd be reading something else. And in the society you live in, money is practically a god, an object of worship.

I'd like to take this opportunity to show you that your

parents, and those who share their views, are actually quite mistaken.

I've repeatedly attempted to explain that we're actually dependent on resources, but no one seems to listen.

Even those who have the Sitting Bull poster with his famous quote in their homes don't seem to grasp its meaning or simply ignore it.

In my natural naivety, I still can't understand why they don't just hand over a credit card to the aspiring Mars colonizers.

If it's true that money can buy anything, why not establish a solid bank account here on Earth, with a reputable bank, and provide the explorers with a few wallets filled with credit cards and cash? Why not offer them some Bitcoins?

Was Sitting Bull right after all? Are plastic cards difficult to digest?

And do you know what the space scientists are experimenting with to prepare for the Mars mission?

With lettuce seedlings!

Come on, it's ridiculous. I can buy a salad at the supermarket for a dollar or two, so why all this fuss to grow it in space?

It's likely because there's no such thing, and if it doesn't exist, you can't buy it, not even with all the gold in the world.

Just as we can't buy the water we need to survive and grow our salad. And just as we can't buy the oxygen we need to live and grow our salad. It's clear that, no matter where we are in the universe, we'll always need these resources, not money. Possessing shares that yield monthly dividends or renting out apartments will never guarantee our survival.

The hominids in Kubrick's film didn't even have a bank

account, just like all the animals on the planet, because they thrived on water, oxygen, and plants that we're destroying in our quest for "wealth".

Teach your children the true value of things, respect for others, and care for the environment.

The true progress and wealth of a people can be seen in this.

Now, since we're already in orbit, let me briefly share the story of the famous moon landing. I don't intend to stir up controversy or take a firm stance. I won't be discussing flags, shadows, or stars. I'm particularly interested in the economic and educational aspects, as well as Kubrick and the assets.
Let me start by saying that it was during the Cold War

era, and both the USSR and the US were vying to prove their superiority and strength. Honor was at stake, and the game was to prove that each ideology was the best (c*******m and capitalism).

The Russians were ahead in technology: they launched the first satellite, sent the first dog into orbit, and put the first man and woman into space. They also created Soyuz, which is still used today, even by Americans and Europeans.
The Americans relied on a German, a former Nazi, who had at least studied something.

While the Russians were comfortably in slippers building robust and reliable technology, the Americans were indulging in cinema and the good life.
And in the movies, we saw people chewing gum, speeding around in sports cars, munching on popcorn, sporting jeans, and sipping whiskey. We saw Kubrick's films, and a plethora of cowboys who were brave and violent, yet as ignorant as cows.

At first glance, we can't help but believe in one version or the other of the moon landing story.

However, there are certain facts that don't require belief, as they're globally recognized.
These facts have slightly influenced my opinion on the credibility of the United States.

Here's the list:

The history of slavery and racial segregation:
For over two centuries, the United States legalized slavery, denying fundamental human rights to millions of people of African descent.
Even after the abolition of slavery, Jim Crow laws enforced racial segregation in southern states, restricting African Americans' access to education, voting, and other civil rights.

The tragic genocide of Native Americans:
The westward expansion of the United States, known as the Far West, led to the systematic extermination and forced removal of Native American populations from their ancestral lands.
Government policies have frequently disregarded treaties and the rights of Native Americans.

Controversial wars and military interventions:
The United States has been involved in numerous controversial wars and military interventions, often driven by economic or geopolitical interests.
Examples include the Vietnam War, the 2003 Iraq invasion, and support for dictatorial regimes in Latin America.

Mass surveillance and privacy breaches:
Following the 9/11 attacks (are you serious???), the United States implemented mass surveillance programs that raised concerns about the privacy of its citizens.
Edward Snowden's revelations, among others, have exposed the extent to which government agencies collect data on a massive scale, often without adequate oversight. And what about Assange, who's been in prison for 12 years...

Restrictions on voting rights:
Throughout history, various groups, including women, African Americans, and Native Americans, have fought for the right to vote.
Even today, discriminatory laws and practices can hinder certain minority groups' access to voting.

Information censorship and control:
During the Cold War, the United States government implemented censorship and propaganda programs to counter the influence of communism.
Even in recent times, there have been instances of journalists and informants being persecuted for disclosing information that was inconvenient to the government.

Election manipulation:
Allegations of manipulation and interference in US elections have been made, both by internal and external actors.
The US electoral system has vulnerabilities that can be exploited to influence the outcome.

I'm not sure if these actions truly reflect the values of those who brandish the torch of freedom (their own, perhaps). Perhaps those who believe in infinite growth are compelled to commit certain crimes.
Perhaps those who can't help but cause disaster feel the need to pretend to be good and capable.
Perhaps the idea of venturing to Mars stems from the realization that we've already destroyed the only habitable planet in our quest for financial freedom.

Uncle Bill's Gardens

After making a fortune with Microsoft, the multibillionaire Bill Gates has also become the largest landowner in the United States.
It's odd that someone like him, who could buy anything he wants, would choose to invest in land. A vast expanse of land, far surpassing that of my grandfather's. Could it be that he knows things we don't?
Well, my grandfather actually knew about it too, and I'm sorry Bill, but he was already aware of it long before you!

And this was already known during the Neolithic era.
In fact, the land has always been the primary source of food and sustenance for the majority of the Earth's population. In the past, agriculture and livestock were the primary economic activities, and it was the possession of fertile land, not money, that ensured survival.

The so-called "Neolithic revolution", which marked the beginning of agriculture and sedentarization around 10,000 years ago, is seen as a pivotal moment in human history.
Cultivating the land has enabled us to produce food more efficiently and predictably than hunting and gathering. This resulted in a greater supply of food and a decrease in hunger-related deaths. Back then, there were no subsidies or grants, and unemployment was a foreign concept.
The increased availability of food has consequently fueled an unprecedented surge in population growth.

Sedentary communities were able to expand, facilitating the division of labor and the emergence of new technologies.

Sedentarization has also enabled the accumulation of goods and resources, such as food, tools, and building materials (and bitcoins). This fostered the emergence of a more complex social structure and new forms of organization.

The increased efficiency of agriculture, as our friend Permaculture is teaching us today, freed up time and energy that could be devoted to other activities, such as crafts, art, and even golf.

The fact that the climate hadn't yet been disrupted by climate change also made it possible to predict natural phenomena with certainty.

Farmers could confidently plan their planting and harvesting, and their understanding of natural cycles, such as the changing seasons, fostered the development of astronomical knowledge and calendars, which were crucial for agriculture and, ultimately, survival.

Humankind also learned to adapt to different climates, developing appropriate agricultural techniques.

Uncle Bill and my grandfather were well aware of all this. And that's why Bill is now heavily investing in extracting CO_2 from the atmosphere.

By relentlessly driving the economy forward through the transportation of goods and people, we are making this planet unpredictable and dangerous. We're shooting ourselves in the foot, in the truest sense of the phrase.

Who knows how much longer we'll be able to witness the seeds sprouting? I wonder if the fruit will have enough time to ripen before winter arrives.

Oh, right, there are underground greenhouses, okay.

Insults and outrage

We're nearing the end of the book, with only the final chapter left to go, the one that will put you face to face with yourself.

If you've made it this far, you've likely grasped the message this book aims to convey. If for some reason you feel offended and believe I've bruised your capitalist pride, or if I've said something uncomfortable that you wish to avoid, feel free to leave a negative review.

I couldn't care less.

I've already experienced this with other unsettling books.

Trolls are always lurking, ready to vent their frustration, and comments are the perfect outlet for them. So go ahead, and remember that your comment, especially if it's negative and destructive, won't change anything. The book, on the other hand, will, because it will remain in print and in circulation.

By the way, I'm now addressing you, Robert. As you know, this is a serious parody, and I have no intention of offending you. In fact, despite not knowing you, I find you likeable after seeing your photo.

I'm aware that uncomfortable realities can often be overshadowed or destroyed. And it's crucial to be wary of those who speak of 'walls of lawyers'.

So, if you or some wealthy golfer with nothing better to do decides to sue, just know that you won't get a penny out of us.

As I'm financially struggling, I won't be able to

compensate you for moral damages, and I don't have any heirs either.

At worst, I'll be forced to go to prison, but at least there, I'll finally get to live at the state's expense without doing anything. Regardless, the book and its ideas will continue to circulate and live on, just as Robin Hood, Che Guevara, Sacco and Vanzetti, Mahatma Gandhi, Nelson Mandela, Martin Luther King, Emmeline Pankhurst, Rosa Parks, Joan of Arc, Spartacus, Pancho Villa, and that unpronounceable evil ideology that begins with C and ends with M have done. Although it's no longer officially alive, it continues to live in many other forms and in the consciousness of millions of people. Those who possess a conscience, naturally.

P.S: I almost forgot to mention something that brings me relief: If we all evaded taxes and were all financially savvy, there probably wouldn't even be prisons. And there wouldn't be any impartial and honest judges to put us on trial.

So, for me, it's all good.

Seeds or ammo?

And here we are, at the final showdown. Here we are, at the chapter that will reveal whether you've enjoyed Robert's book more or this pile of nonsense written by a moron.

As the chapter's title perfectly conveys, we're at a crossroads. Soon, whether you like it or not, you'll have to make a choice for yourself and your children.

It appears that, as things are currently unfolding, a widespread collapse of our society is imminent. As you know, this has already happened a few times in human history. For one reason or another, things cease to function, and from an organized and predictable state, we enter a highly unstable and out-of-control era.
Everyone strives to save themselves and survive as best they can, using the resources at their disposal.
I'm not one of those people who predict 18 months of total anarchy (I don't know why 18) immediately after a blackout, for example, or a catastrophe so severe that it brings the "civilized" world to its knees.
But let's imagine that it actually happens.
Imagine a scenario where an earthquake or a storm leaves a large part of the territory without electricity, water, and all the things we take for granted. Just a month ago in Valencia, Spain, a similar event unfolded. People emptied a couple of supermarkets in the blink of an eye.

Which side will you choose?
Will you choose to loot or join forces with others?
To steal or to cultivate?
Should we rebuild or finish destroying?

Mors tua vita mea?

In conclusion...

I sincerely hope that your children won't turn into ruthless and violent gunmen.

I hope you can proudly look them in the eye when they ask you what you do and how you make a living.

I hope they can access a quality education and live a healthy life in a healthy society.

I hope you can continue to take them on long walks, exploring the wonders of this planet.

I hope you never see them go hungry.

I hope you'll only see them dressed as cowboy during carnival...

*Satire, environment and education.
All in one.*

www.ingramcontent.com/pod-product-compliance
Lightning Source LLC
Chambersburg PA
CBHW070956240526
45469CB00016B/1338